Dear Parents and Educators,

Welcome to Penguin Young Readers! As parents and educators, you know that each child develops at their own pace—in terms of speech, critical thinking, and, of course, reading. Penguin Young Readers recognizes this fact. As a result, each Penguin Young Readers book is assigned a traditional easy-to-read level (1–4) ~~ ~~ ''
F&P Text Level (A–R). Both of these
right book for your child. Please refe
for specific leveling information. Pen
esteemed authors and illustrators, sto
fascinating nonfiction, and more!

Are Sea Monsters Real?	LEVEL **4**
	F&P TEXT LEVEL **R**

This book is perfect for a **Fluent Reader** who:
- can read the text quickly with minimal effort;
- has good comprehension skills;
- can self-correct (can recognize when something doesn't sound right); and
- can read aloud smoothly and with expression.

Here are some **activities** you can do during and after reading this book:
- Creative Writing: At the end of the book, the author writes: "But many surprising sea creatures are out there—some yet to be discovered. Maybe you will find them!" Write a paragraph describing a new sea monster that you could imagine discovering out in the ocean. What does it look like? How does it act? Where does it live?
- Comprehension: After reading the book, answer the following questions:
  - How big is the kraken, according to legends?
  - What are the names of the two Greek sea monsters?
  - What country is the Loch Ness monster from?
  - What is the only predator of the giant squid?
  - Which ancient shark's name means "great tooth"?

Remember, sharing the love of reading with a child is the best gift you can give!

*This book has been officially leveled by using the F&P Text Level Gradient™ leveling system.

For Pamela S. Johnson, my former
professor and mentor and a wonderful friend:
thanks for showing me the beauty in the
everyday and the possibilities for
art everywhere—GLC

PENGUIN YOUNG READERS
An imprint of Penguin Random House LLC, New York

First published in the United States of America by Penguin Young Readers,
an imprint of Penguin Random House LLC, New York, 2022

Photo credits: used throughout: (photo frame) happyfoto/E+/Getty Images, (torn paper) jayk7/Moment/Getty Images; cover, 3: Mathias Berger/iStock/Getty Images; 4–5: SergeyMikhaylov/iStock/Getty Images; 6: IADA/iStock/Getty Images; 7, 10–11, 15, 16–17: duncan1890/DigitalVision Vectors/Getty Images; 8: ivan-96/iStock/Getty Images; 9: JonnyJim/iStock/Getty Images; 12: ZU_09/DigitalVision Vectors/Getty Images; 13: Science History Images/Alamy Stock Photo; 14: (frame) TomekD76/iStock/Getty Images, (sea serpent reported by Hans Egede; illustration from *Norges Naturlige Historie* by Erik Pontoppidan) public domain, via Wikimedia Commons; 18–19: MR1805/iStock/Getty Images; 19: (Loch Ness monster) Matt84/E+/Getty Images; 20–21: Josef Hanus/Alamy Stock Photo; 22: benoitb/DigitalVision Vectors/Getty Images; 23: (giant squid beak, National Museum of Ireland – Natural History) Mgiganteus1, via Wikimedia Commons (CC BY-SA 4.0); 24: Dorling Kindersley/Getty Images; 25: hlansdown/iStock/Getty Images; 26: WhitcombeRD/iStock/Getty Images; 27: karen crewe/iStock/Getty Images; 28–29, 44: dottedhippo/iStock/Getty Images; 30: Rebecca-Belleni-Photography/iStock/Getty Images; 31: DEA/G. ROLI/De Agostini/Getty Images; 32: Grafissimo/E+/Getty Images; 33: by wildestanimal/Moment/Getty Images; 34–35: Comstock Images/Stockbyte/Getty Images; 35: (Steller's sea cow) THEPALMER/DigitalVision Vectors/Getty Images; 36: Zocha_K/E+/Getty Images; 37: slowmotiongli/iStock/Getty Images; 38: kool99/iStock/Getty Images; 39: MR1805/iStock/Getty Images; 40: Roland Bouvier/Alamy Stock Photo; 41: CoreyFord/iStock/Getty Images; 42–43: mikroman6/Moment/Getty Images; 45: (*Basilosaurus*, Field Museum, Chicago) Amphibol, via Wikimedia Commons (CC BY-SA 4.0); 46: Warpaintcobra/iStock/Getty Images; 47: Mark Kostich/iStock/Getty Images; 48: Kenkola/iStock/Getty Images

Visit us online at penguinrandomhouse.com.

Library of Congress Cataloging-in-Publication Data is available.

Manufactured in China

ISBN 9780593383933 (pbk)   10 9 8 7 6 5 4 3 2 1 WKT
ISBN 9780593383940 (hc)   10 9 8 7 6 5 4 3 2 1 WKT

ARE
SEA MONSTERS
REAL?

by Ginjer L. Clarke

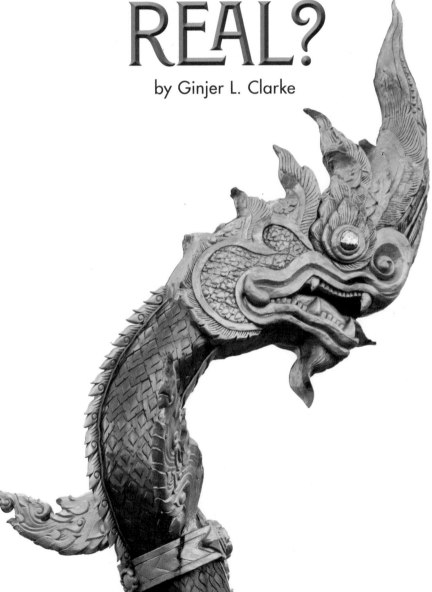

What Is a Sea Monster?

A monster can be any large, scary
creature. A sea monster is even scarier.
It hides in deep, dark waters that hold
many mysteries.

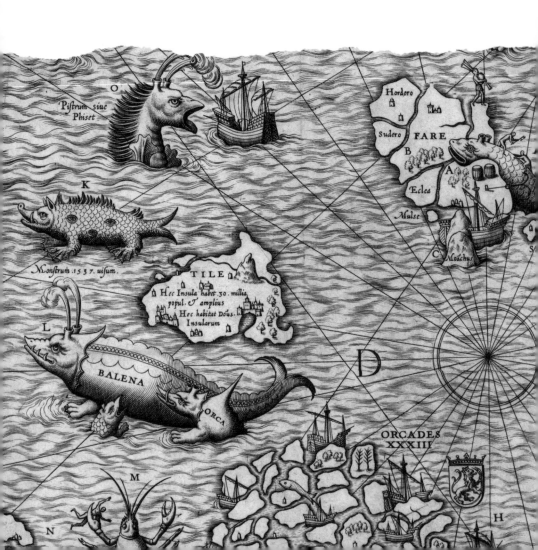

Long ago, fishermen and sailors feared unknown sea creatures. They believed these monsters would sink their ships and eat them!

Today, we know many of the fearsome stories they believed can be explained. But some real sea creatures are true monsters of the deep!

Sea Monster Stories and Art

The word *kraken* (say: CRACK-en) means a "fabulous sea monster" from Norway. The story of the kraken is at least 500 years old.

One writer from Norway said the kraken was more than a mile long—as big as an island. It had many arms that were as long as a ship is tall.

Slurp! Sailors believed the kraken pulled down a ship by making a swirling whirlpool. *Gulp!* One story said the kraken ate whales—in a single bite!

The kraken was big, but the leviathan (say: luh-VY-eh-thin) was massive. Tales of the leviathan were in two books of religious stories, the Jewish Talmud and the Christian Bible. They said the leviathan was hundreds of miles long! It was called the "dragon of the sea."

The leviathan acted like a dragon, too. *Whoosh!* It had terrible teeth, breathed fire, and blew smoke. *Swoosh!* It even made the ocean water boil!

Another sea monster from Norway was the Midgard serpent. This serpent was so large that it created storms in the ocean when it swam. *Crash!*

One legend said the Midgard serpent once battled Thor, the god of thunder.

The serpent was almost killed, and now
it hides in the sea. The story says the
great serpent will rise up again one day.
Smash! Thor will finally defeat it, but he
will die, too.

The hero Odysseus (say: oh-DISS-ee-us) battled a very scary sea monster in an ancient Greek story. He had to sail his boat past Scylla (say: SILL-uh). She had six heads with sharp teeth! She lived in a cave and grabbed sailors out of boats that dared to pass by her.

In another tale, the hero Hercules fought the hydra, which was also a cave serpent with many heads. But each time he cut off one head, two more would grow back!

Sea Monster Sightings

Not all sea monster stories are tales from long ago. Many real people have reported seeing sea serpents all around the world.

One famous sighting happened on a boat sailing to Greenland in 1734. "Look!" The people on the boat pointed and shouted. A writer said they saw "a very terrible sea animal" with a body like a snake and a head like a whale.

Many pictures were drawn of this sea serpent. People still argue today about what creature it could have been.

Another true sea monster sighting was of a brown, snaky beast with a horse-like head. It swam fast, moving up and down like a caterpillar. It was seen a lot off the coast of Massachusetts, from 1817 until the early 1900s.

The captain of a British ship sailing off the coast of Africa in August 1848 described a similar creature. Many people thought this sea monster might be a type of swimming dinosaur that was supposed to be extinct. Wow!

The most famous and most loved sea monster is probably Nessie, the Loch Ness monster. It is said to have a large, humped body with a long neck and a small head. Stories say it lives in an underground cave of a deep lake in Scotland near a castle.

People have said they spotted this creature many times for hundreds of years. In 1934, a doctor said he took a photo of Nessie, but it turned out to be fake. Scientists have looked for proof, but no one knows if Nessie truly exists.

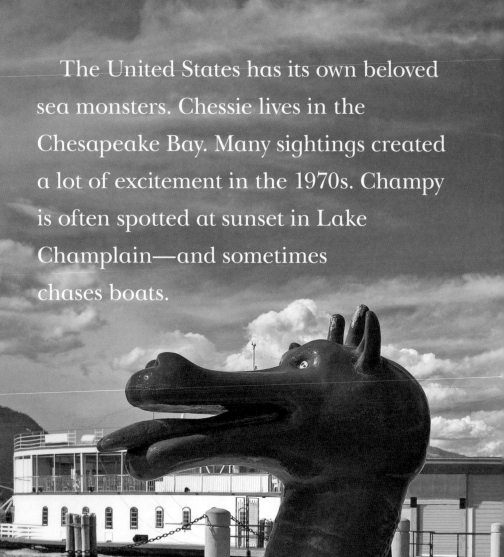

The United States has its own beloved sea monsters. Chessie lives in the Chesapeake Bay. Many sightings created a lot of excitement in the 1970s. Champy is often spotted at sunset in Lake Champlain—and sometimes chases boats.

Sculpture of Lake Okanagan sea monster Ogopogo

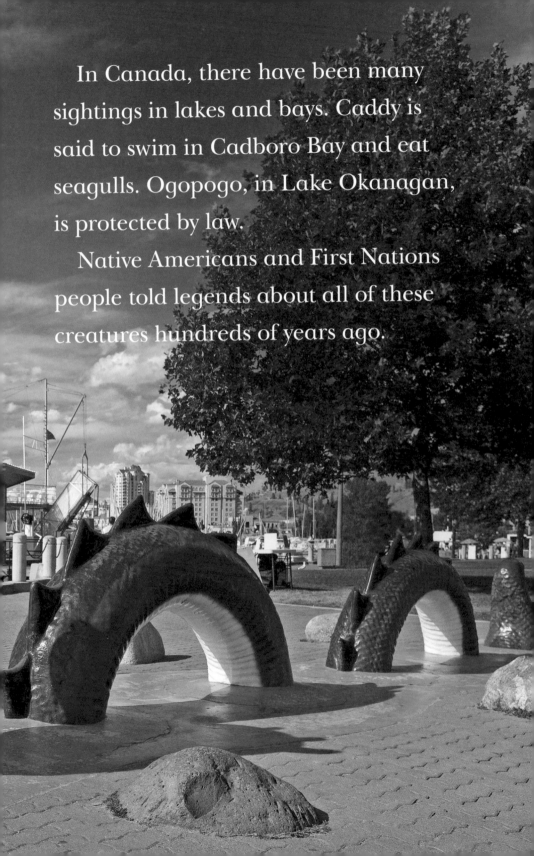

In Canada, there have been many sightings in lakes and bays. Caddy is said to swim in Cadboro Bay and eat seagulls. Ogopogo, in Lake Okanagan, is protected by law.

Native Americans and First Nations people told legends about all of these creatures hundreds of years ago.

Real-Life Sea Monsters

Are any of these sea monster stories and sightings true? Yes! The giant squid is the real creature that Scylla, the kraken, the sea serpent, and more were based on.

This amazing deep-sea animal does not sink ships like the kraken, but it does

eat whales! The giant squid wraps its 30-foot-long tentacles around a whale and squeezes tightly. *Crunch!* It bites its prey into pieces with its powerful beak. *Munch!* It eats with its sharp tongue covered in tiny teeth.

Giant squid beak

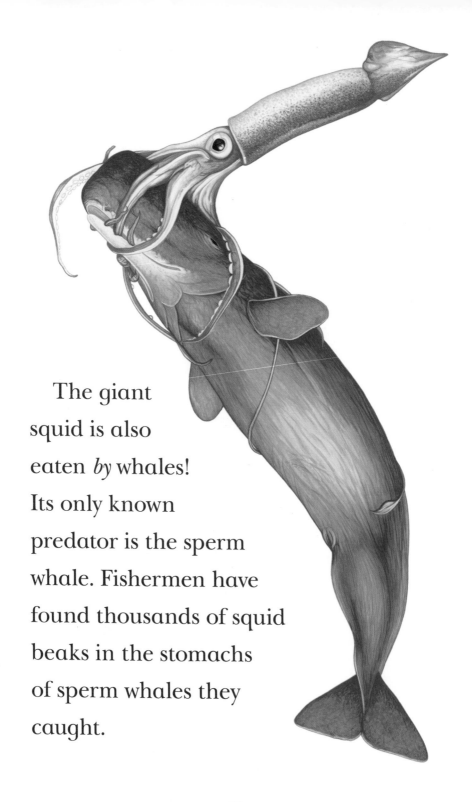

The giant
squid is also
eaten *by* whales!
Its only known
predator is the sperm
whale. Fishermen have
found thousands of squid
beaks in the stomachs
of sperm whales they
caught.

The sperm whale does sometimes attack ships when it is being hunted. It weighs about the same as seven elephants, making it the largest hunter on Earth!

The sperm whale's enormous size and ability to spout air that looks like smoke may have created the legend of the leviathan.

The story of the hydra may have been inspired by the giant Pacific octopus. It can regrow any of its eight arms if they are broken. What a handy trick!

This largest of all octopuses was once called the "devil fish." It was greatly feared but not fully understood.

It is big enough to wrap its arms
around a small car. And it has a fierce
look in its eyes. But the giant octopus is
actually very smart, shy, and gentle—
except to the shellfish it eats.

A true sea serpent is the oarfish. This shiny silver fish can be at least 40 feet long—about the length of a tractor trailer. That makes it the longest bony fish alive today!
It has a spiny
red mane

running along the top of its eel-like body.
   This odd feature might explain why
many sea monsters were described as
having the head of a horse and the
body of a snake. Although the deep-sea
oarfish is rarely seen, it is very real!

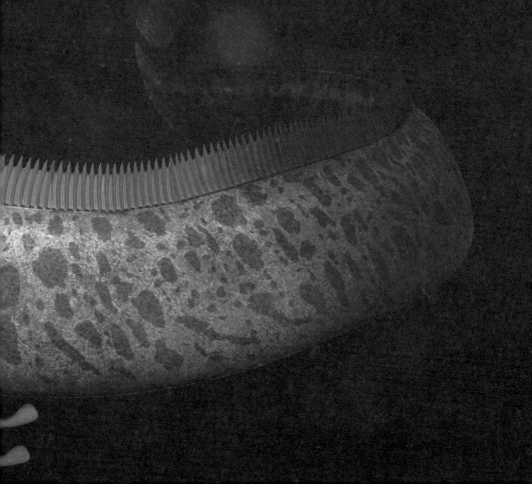

Wannabe Sea Monsters

The basking shark is clearly a shark when it is alive. But it has sometimes been mistaken for a sea monster when it is found dead.

The basking shark is the second largest shark, after the whale shark.

Scoop! It opens its massive mouth and sucks up thousands of tiny plankton.

Floop! But when this shark dies, its head and body look much smaller. Some creatures that seemed to be sea serpents were later proven to be dead basking sharks.

Are killer whales, or orcas, really whales? No! Orcas hunt whales, so they could be called "whale killers," but they are actually dolphins.

Orcas are definitely sea monsters— at least to other sea creatures! They are the top ocean predators, and they eat anything they can catch.

Orcas work together in groups called pods. *Click! Clack!* They talk to each other using special sounds. *Swirl! Whirl!* They circle around their prey and trap it before attacking.

Many
stories have
been written
about mermaids.
Did you know that
mermaids are based on a real
animal, the manatee?

The manatee is not a beautiful half-woman with long, flowing hair. But it is a graceful swimmer with a human-like body and a fishy tail.

The Steller's sea cow was a larger cousin of the manatee. It is now extinct, but it inspired many mermaid tales, too. The explorer Christopher Columbus even thought he saw three mermaids in 1493, but they were really manatees!

The sturgeon (say: STIR-jun) is a giant, ancient fish that grows up to 20 feet long. It has been around since the time of dinosaurs! This monster travels from the sea into rivers. Its bumpy back and wiggly motion make it a true sea serpent.

The coelacanth (say: SEAL-eh-kanth) fish also lived long ago. Scientists believed it was extinct, but one was found alive in 1938! Now some people wonder what other ancient creatures might still be hiding in the oceans.

Ancient Sea Monsters

The largest sea monsters ever lived long, long ago. *Dunkleosteus* (say: dun-kul-OS-tee-us) was the biggest ocean creature before the time of dinosaurs. Its original name meant "terrible fish."

Bang! Clang! Dunkleosteus had a hard head covered in bony plates to protect it in fights. It had the strongest jaws of any fish ever. *Slice! Dice!* Its super-sharp jaws cut a shark in half like scissors. It could have crushed a human like a bug!

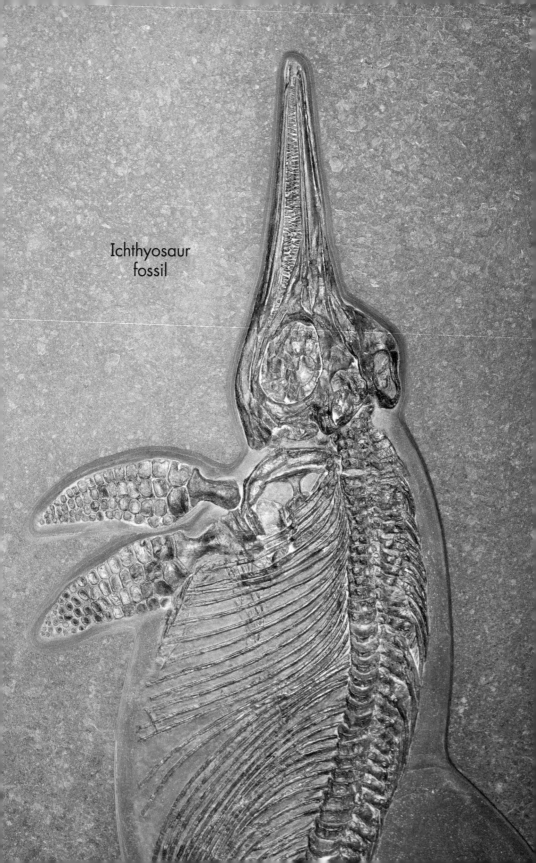

Ichthyosaur
fossil

Some of the largest sea monsters were ichthyosaurs (say: ICK-thee-oh-sawrz), or "fish-lizards." *Cymbospondylus* (say: sim-bow-SPOND-ee-lus) was one type of ichthyosaur. It was a fast, powerful swimmer. *Zoom!* It looked like a huge dolphin with a long tail.

Another ichthyosaur, *Shonisaurus* (say: SHOW-neh-SAWR-us), was once the largest animal on Earth—as long as two school buses. It could see in dark water with its big eyes. *Boom!* It grabbed a *Cymbospondylus* with its long snout and pointy teeth.

Other giant sea monsters were the plesiosaurs (say: PLEEZ-ee-oh-sawrz), or "almost lizards." *Elasmosaurus* (say: eh-LAZZ-mo-SAWR-us) was a long-necked plesiosaur. It looked just like Nessie!

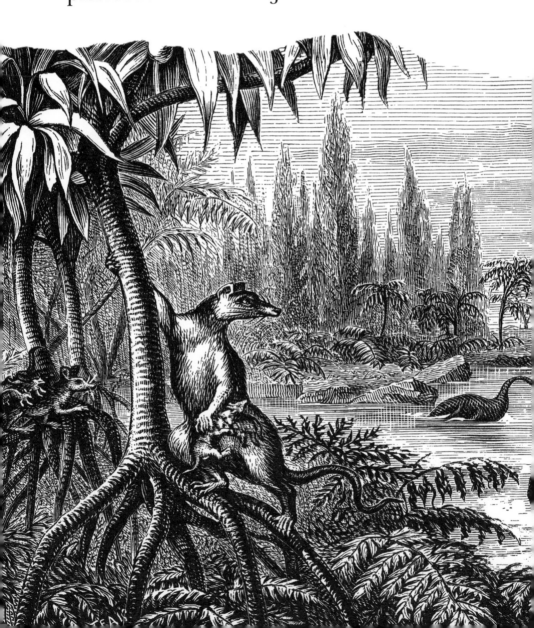

Liopleurodon (say: LIE-oh-PLOOR-oh-don) was a short-necked plesiosaur. It was possibly the scariest sea creature of all time. *Thrash!* It whipped a shark from side to side. *Mash!* It ripped apart its prey with jaws that were stronger than those of a *Tyrannosaurus rex*.

Basilosaurus (say: BASS-il-oh-SAWR-us) means "king lizard." But it was actually an ocean mammal like a whale. It grew up to 70 feet long. That's about as long as four giraffes stacked on top of each other!

A scientist once thought it was even bigger, but it turned out he had put

together the bones from two different *Basilosaurus* skeletons. Whoops!

This monster was no gentle giant like most of today's whales. *Whip! Basilosaurus* caught a squid with its sharp, cone-shaped teeth. *Rip!* Then it shredded its prey with its larger back teeth.

Megalodon (say: MEG-uh-la-don) means "great tooth." A megalodon shark tooth was almost three times bigger than the tooth of a great white shark. Sharks lose teeth constantly as they grow new ones.

Giant megalodon teeth have been found
all over the world.

Megalodon was the largest and most
dangerous shark that ever lived. It would
have been five times heavier than a
Tyrannosaurus rex! It was the scariest sea
monster of all time.

The world's oceans
are huge and hold
lots of mysteries. Sea
monsters in stories
from the past may
not be real. But many
surprising sea creatures
are out there—some
yet to be discovered.
Maybe you will
find them!